Mary Anderson
and Windshield Wipers

By Ellen Labrecque

21st Century
Junior Library

Published in the United States of America by
Cherry Lake Publishing
Ann Arbor, Michigan
www.cherrylakepublishing.com

Content Adviser: Amelia Wenk Gotwals, Ph.D., Associate Professor of Science Education, Michigan State University
Reading Adviser: Marla Conn MS, Ed., Literacy specialist, Read-Ability, Inc.

Photo Credits: © Dark Moon Pictures/Shutterstock Images, cover, 20; © ambrozinio/Shutterstock Images, 4;
©Detroit Publishing Co./Library of Congress, 6; ©Everett Historical/Shutterstock Images, 8; © Harris & Ewing/Library of
Congress, 10; © May Anderson (743801)/United Sates Patent and Trademark Office/National Archives and Records
Administration, 12; © Alexander Mitrofanov/Dreamstime, 14; © alexsvirid/Shutterstock Images, 16; © Ditty_about_summer/
Shutterstock Images, 18

Library of Congress Cataloging-in-Publication Data
Names: Labrecque, Ellen, author.
Title: Mary Anderson and windshield wipers / by Ellen Labrecque. Other titles: 21st century junior library.
Description: Ann Arbor : Cherry Lake Publishing, [2017] | Series: 21st century junior library | Series: Women innovators | Includes
    bibliographical references and index.
Identifiers: LCCN 2016029713 | ISBN 9781634721783 (hardcover) | ISBN 9781634723107 (pbk.) | ISBN 9781634722445 (pdf) |
    ISBN 9781634723763 (ebook)
Subjects: LCSH: Anderson, Mary, 1866-1953–Juvenile literature. | Windshield wipers–Juvenile literature. | Women inventors–
    United States–Biography–Juvenile literature. | Inventors–United States–Biography–Juvenile literature.
Classification: LCC T40.A53 L33 2017 | DDC 629.2/76 [B]–dc23
LC record available at https://lccn.loc.gov/2016029713

Cherry Lake Publishing would like to acknowledge the work of The Partnership for 21st Century Skills.
Please visit www.p21.org for more information.

Printed in the United States of America
Corporate Graphics

CONTENTS

It is important for drivers to be able to see in all kinds of weather.

A Woman

Have you ever ridden in a car when it is raining? The rain is coming down hard. But the driver can still see through the **windshield**! Swish! Swash! Rain and snow are wiped away.

Mary Anderson **invented** the **windshield wiper** more than 100 years ago!

In Birmingham, Anderson became an **entrepreneurial** woman.

Mary Anderson was born on February 19, 1866, in Greene County, Alabama. Her dad died when she was four years old. When she was a young adult, she moved to Birmingham, Alabama, with her mom and sister. They built an apartment complex. They rented apartments to people and also lived there.

Before buses, many towns had trolley cars.

In the winter of 1902, Anderson visited New York City. On a snowy day, she noticed that **trolley car** drivers struggled to see through their windshields. Drivers would stop their trolleys to get out and clean their windshields by hand. Others would open their windshields, exposing themselves to the snow. Some drivers even leaned out the side to see properly. Anderson couldn't believe it. She thought there should be a safer and better way to drive during a snowstorm.

Anderson hoped her invention would be used on
trolley car windows like this one.

An Idea

Anderson went home. She sketched an idea for a wiper that would clear away snow and rain. It operated by a lever on the inside of the car. The driver pulled the lever. Then the wiper moved back and forth in a fanning motion. A rubber blade wiped away rain and snow from the window.

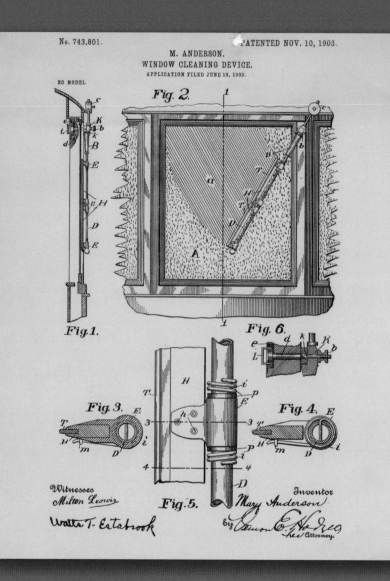

To get her patent, Anderson made detailed drawings of her invention.

Anderson had a model of her design made. Her idea was **patented** on November 10, 1903. On the patent, she described her invention as "a window cleaning device for electric cars and other vehicles to remove snow, ice, and sleet from the window."

Look!

Look at this drawing of Anderson's windshield wiper. Is the wiper the same as the ones that cars have today? How is it different?

In 1903, most cars looked like this Ford Model T.

Anderson tried to sell her wiper idea to different companies. But nobody wanted to buy it. At the time, there weren't many cars on the road. The cars that were on the road didn't have roofs. People didn't drive in rain or snow. Anderson let her patent **expire** in 1920.

Think!

Would Anderson's invention have been a success if she had invented it at a later time in history? Why or why not?

As cars became more popular in the 1920s,
new windshield wipers were developed.

A Legacy

Soon after Anderson let her patent expire, another person patented a similar windshield wiper design. This was the one that was eventually adopted for cars. Anderson died in 1953 at the age of 86. She never earned any money from her invention. But her **legacy** is that she is recognized as the first person to invent windshield wipers.

Windshield wipers have improved over the years,
but their purpose remains the same.

Windshield wipers have come a long way since Anderson's day. They work at the push of a button. Rain-sensing wipers turn on or off, speed up or slow down, depending on how hard the rain is falling. Wipers now clear off airplanes and space shuttle windows, too!

Create!

Create a new design for windshield wipers. Draw and describe your design. Which way do the wipers move? How does the driver start them? Consider adding snow or fog control to your design. How would those features work?

Today, windshield wipers are one of many important devices that keep us safe on the road.

Anderson did not become famous or rich for inventing the windshield wiper. But she saw a need for an invention and did something about it. She is an inventor in every sense of the word!

GLOSSARY

entrepreneurial (ahn-truh-pruh-NUR-ee-uhl) interested in starting a business and finding new ways to make money

expire (ik-SPIRE) to reach the end of the time when something can be legally or properly used

invented (in-VENT-id) created something new from imagination

legacy (LEG-uh-see) something handed down from one generation to another

patented (PAT-uhn-tid) obtained the right from the government to use or sell an invention for a certain number of years

trolley car (TRAH-ee KAHR) a streetcar powered by electricity that operates on a track

windshield (WIND-sheeld) a window of glass protecting the front of a vehicle

windshield wiper (WIND-sheeld WYE-pur) a device designed to wipe away snow, rain, and sleet

FIND OUT MORE

BOOKS

Indovino, Shaina. *Women Inventors*. Broomall, PA: Mason Crest, 2014.

Latta, Sara. *The Woman Who Invented Windshield Wipers*: *Mary Anderson and Her Wonderful Invention*. Berkeley Heights, NJ: Enslow Elementary: 2014.

Thimmesh, Catherine. *Girls Think of Everything: Stories of Ingenious Inventions by Women*. Boston: Houghton Mifflin Company, 2000.

WEB SITES

Famous Women Inventors
www.women-inventors.com/Mary-Anderson.asp
Another great site to learn about Anderson and other women inventors.

National Inventors Hall of Fame
http://invent.org/inductee-detail/?IID=422
Read all about Anderson and other great inventors.

INDEX

ABOUT THE AUTHOR

Ellen Labrecque is a freelance writer living in Yardley, Pennsylvania. Previously, she was a senior editor at Sports Illustrated Kids. Ellen loves to travel and then learn about new places and people that she can write about in her books.